Wayward Poet

Wayward Poet

JAN McGRATH

Illustrations by
ANITA BENSON

Epigraph Books
Rhinebeck, New York

Wayward Poet © Copyright 2023 by Jan McGrath

All rights reserved. No part of this book may be used or reproduced in any manner without the consent of the author except in critical articles or reviews. Contact the publisher for information.

ISBN 978-1-960090-29-4

Library of Congress Control Number 2023914440

Illustrations and cover art by Anita Benson
Book design by Colin Rolfe

Epigraph Books
22 East Market Street, Suite 304
Rhinebeck, New York 12572
(845) 876-4861
epigraphps.com

*for Mom, Dad, and Eileen
who first laid out a path for me~*

*and for my son John Narayan Shiarella
who has lighted my way on it ever since~
with Aleksandra, AJ, Jessica and Andrew, and Zara.*

CONTENTS

Foreword   xi

Families

of Origin
- Family Album   3
- Family Album II   5
- Family Album VII   6
- Our Steps   7
- Honor   8
- Without End   9
- Epilogue   11
- Parking Lot   12
- To the Lions   13
- Nana   14
- Dichotomy   15

of Progeny
- Bond   17
- Apologia II   18
- Testament   20
- Exchange   21
- Algorithm   22
- 5th Command   23
- Helpmate   24
- Artemis of the Playground   25
- Commencement   26
- Prospecting   27
- Legacy   28
- The Smoothers   29

Loves

Cocktail Party	33
White Elephants	34
Trip	35
Green Lilacs	36
Spring	37
Parallel Lines	38
Mind's Eyes	39
In Concert	41
Breakfast	42
Communication	43
Red Stamps	44
For Such a Man	45
2000 Days	46
My Maine	48
Options	49
Friday Lost	50
Pan, Unmasked	51
The Rock	52
Light	53
Mediation: Heron	54
Settled In	55
Seedbed	56

Worlds

Hometown

Irish Ides	59
October Nightmare	61
Requiescat	62

Kenya

Kwa Heri	63

Hygiene	64
Dragonflies	65
They	66
Town Boys, Uganda	67
Verse and Response	68
The Norfolk	70

Maine

Inhabitants	71
The Auction	73
Pine Groves	77
Round Pond	78

Here

The Aina	79
Faith	80
Sideswiped	81
Orchestration	82

Reflections

Warmups

Transformation	85
True Love	85
Coast Town	85
Beachgoers	85
Quelle?	85
Teen Spring	85

Portraits

First Day	86
Life Study, Sam	87
Resilience	88
Grace	89
Pre-Post Prandial	90
Swimmer	91
To an Analyst	92

Emperorang	93
Imported Beauty's Vow	94
Shoddy Product	95
Energy Crisis	96
Waterborne	97
Zara, Year One	99
Ponderings	
Reply to Bobby Burns	100
Exposure	101
Proprietary Rights	102
Exempt	103
Universal Blessing	104
About the Author and Illustrator	105
Acknowledgments	107

Foreword

Since my childhood growing up in the Hudson Valley, I've loved many things~nature, animals and people, and books~all reading really, but especially poetry. I wrote it as well in those years, when the spirit moved me. But it was East Africa and poet Angus Calder's mentoring that fired the urgency in me to keep recording my thoughts and experiences in poems. As I did, I had no idea that, as some do with photographs, I was preserving memories.

Relationships, familial and forged, were the most important inspirations. Places, not just visited but lived in, contributed their voices to my own, while joys and disappointments clamored to be heard. So it appears that this collection, slivers from so many decades of writing, serves as a sort of lifelong journal in verse, happily relieving me of any obligation to ever write a memoir.

Jan McGrath
Kailua, Hawaii
July, 2023

*"The great thing about getting older is
that you don't lose all the other ages you've been."*
                                         Madeleine L'Engle

Families

of Origin

of Progeny

OF ORIGIN

Family Album

Her body filled the doorway
and the smells my nose
of sachets lavender
and rhubarb stewed.

Great empty house
all spit and polished
with ammonia wash and lemon wax,
stairs curving down
to big piano never played,
and in the parlor
antimacassars that I knew
spawned others
though I spied in vain
to see one born.
Rich burgundy upholstery
deceptive velvet-like
that itched the backs of summer legs.

But most of all the prisms,
those great crystal prisms,
shutting out their
"who she married"
"one of the Green Island Baileys
not the Troy branch"
into just absurdity.
And so it was,
because the only real world
was one street in Watervliet

turned blue-gold-purple
by the magic glass
in this the great aunt's house
I hated visiting
except the prisms.

How my uncle barely said a word
except when prodded
"As I always say to Ed"
"Didn't I say that, Ed?"
Her owl's head turning, turning,
Always him to verify
"Yes, Carrie."
White-haired, over-whittled
model of a man--her vassal.
Yet I wonder now
had he died first,
would she not have been shattered.
What if she'd turned and turned
and found no one to verify
"Didn't I say that?
Didn't I say that?
Didn't I say that…?"
Prism, tell.
Was she his rock or was he hers?
Oh, prism, truth.

"Well, didn't I say that, Ed?"
"Yes, Carrie."

Family Album II

"Bonjour, Memere" we thought meant grandma but did not
linoleum floors and rag rugs scattered
clock with the pendulum ticking away
room overheated from stove with kerosene,

The kitchen where we sat in rocking chairs
(One day I'll have a kitchen with two rocking chairs
I've favored kitchen conversation ever since).
An air raid drill, the blackout
and a warden in the white hat, checking
"Evening, Celina, all right here?"
Sitting still in fear it might be real
and in excitement knowing it would not.

A few times sleeping there, the chamber pots
although there was an inside toilet.
Never woke up in the night at home
but here at least six times to savor
all the fun of sitting on the round, cold
nicely fitted bowl and with a night light
we insisted was necessity, she knew was not
but let us have it nonetheless.
I wonder whether she too feared the dark
and liked the comfort of that light
throughout the lonely years
without her husband in a world of twos.

Family Album VII

Mostly I see him at work in our kitchen
cooking a two hour late supper snack
the windows too-laden with billows of smoke
from potatoes he charred in the mounds of black grease
while he scaled out the bullheads he'd caught on the waterfront,

Treating us likely the hundred tenth time
to the tale of his capturing San Juan with Teddy
but undoubtedly spent the whole time peeling spuds
in that war that was not a war, soldier unsoldierly.

Following then to the basement room with him
to musty old man smells of beer and tobacco
of fishing gear sodden not salt sea but river mud,
him rolling cigarettes molded with spittle,
the two digitalis pills close by his side.

We two like old pals watching TV
with Gorgeous George wrestling,
me laughing to see for the first time a faker
a funnier phony than my good old Pop.

Our Steps

Breakfasts--
all of the breakfasts past
so many mornings
locked in his gait

Needs of the moment
needs of a few
but four thousand mornings
locked in his gait

Stumbles and trembles
longings once felt
memorized mornings
locked in his gait

Comforts and kisses
echoes of time
and mornings on mornings
linked to his gait

Never tomorrow
only the past
of myriad mornings
lost with his gait.

Honor

The tabloids claim Chris Reeve may choose to die.
But he has children.
And my mind flies back half-century to us…

I waltz perched on your feet
and on your shoulders sail around the icy lake;
In summer there play porpoise on your back.
"Oh, there goes Earl Champagne… Hey, Champ!"
Revered, endeared, and never still,
those few quick years of early me.

Then suddenly to see you felled. Impossible.
"Now if he falls, protect his head, honey."
A year, two years, no tennis, no more seizures.

"Honey, look. See Daddy wiggle his left toe."
It doesn't—but I giggle as your eyes grin
and your eyebrows wiggle, laughing still
at Baby Snooks, Red Skelton. Teasing,
playing animal or vegetable or mineral.

All those months in that big bed, each hour must
have seemed a hundred days to your expansive heart
with just us there, the radio, the God
whom some would say betrayed you, yet you trusted.

And it wonders me, has served me all my life
you chose to honor us and stay, so joyfully.

Without End

a-men (a-without + men)

They said that night my Memere touched the body,
wiped the sweat she thought was on his lip,
so we were told about it in the morning.
Heads shook, lips pursed, such a lack of dignity
and we agreed not thinking for a second of her feelings
for who knew at twelve the pain a mother of a grown man bore.

They mustered calm and took us out.
My mother stayed inside for she the privileged
had her final private moment with him,
and I often after wondered how she'd used it.

We gathered at the cars.
All eyes and minds including mine
were focused on Memere and Pepere,
death forgotten in the intrigue,
satisfied when my Memere refused
to share a car with him, to put the son
she'd borne and took away from him
out of his reach for good.

But grey smooth men in grey smooth coats
Stepped in and brought another car.
My mother came at last,
black garb now on her face as well with veiling
separating her from us in color too
for she'd refused to blacken us.

We countered her with darkest blue,
correct for little girls to mourn before their time,
the hues combined in homage to our state of hearts.

The church's stifling lack of air muted the shutter clicking
in my mind, but going out again
the bearers all were weeping, all those men
I never knew could cry, and couldn't I suppose,
except they loved him so and saw their lives
like ours diminished from that moment on.

The graveyard was so cold, such dirty snow,
it wondered me how they had dug that ground,
so hard and yet so neatly,
but since they had worked for him and with him,
he belonged to them as well,
so in the frigid earth each corner of his grave
was etched impeccably for love of him.

I cannot quite recall the throwing of the earth
except the priest his friend was weeping
and I know in duty I contributed to both.

But ever since, remembering the bleakness
as we three rode home, the emptiness ahead
when all the grey smooth men had gone away,
I know the moment--any moment--of interment
is what I most dread about the deadly ritual,
for as a coffin's lowered, somewhere in my mind
I hear the echoed mockery of our life ahead
our world of years to be --A men.

Epilogue

The funeral done, the family gone,
to suffer less abruptly all the absence
he had left us in our house,
we spent two weeks upstate
at aunt and uncle's in the country.

The uncle whom I tried to substitute,
uncomfortable with obsession
or perhaps with prepubescence
nudged me gently off his knee.

So on that night before returning home
I woke and went outside to be with me
and hope to feel my father's presence.

I do not know what 3AM may signify
although I still awaken then
but all the same it was the time
and I was savoring the sky and me alone
when she appeared.

And I suppose that she was frightened
by my being gone,
but she intruded on the ease of solitude
I was to seek for years
and might have conquered,
had she left me for that single time I needed
to confront my singularity.

Parking Lot

Rain dwindling, lingering damp
I sip the now cold coffee, turn the engine on,
back out, defroster whirring.

Grey and white cars, wet asphalt
but there ahead the bright pair
rooster, red and gold; his hen, all gold
yet still the royal pace behind.

My smile stays, driving forward
till I see him there
no longer yellow fuzzed
but mini-appaloosa speckled, head turn-turning.
Oh, poor baby, lost your mom--- She's back there.

And, as suddenly---the memory.
But you were always there,
there when I needed you,
so often, though, when I did not.

The week he died you found me in the yard
the middle of the night of solitude, of seeking,
but that moment--
all the later moments flood in
of my shrugs, curt brushings off--

It never crossed my mind
you may have needed me.

To the Lions

She haunts me standing there that day
her world inconsequential, all bedraggled.
The sweat of August in July,
the pallor of a grievous marriage all foreseen
forlorn, reflected in her eyes, as gently so
she leaned, so gently, ironing the pink chiffon
herself to save it scorching—so unlike
the pale blue lace the mother pressed for her
too many years before, too different from two
daughters veiling eyes of pity and relief.

But pink chiffon, unwishful, too unvirginal
would yet encase her that next first day
and the sun of August in July, too orange,
would clash against the pink chiffon
and turn it into irons scorching her,
unwishful, too unvirginal--- belated irons,
fettering her to her martyrdom.

Nana

Her dreary time behind her,
a tea lady, true, she is
not quite the women's Koffee Klatch-mate
although viewed by those with admiration,
not so by the children
(who eschew the admiration thing
leaning to pure aversion or to adoration).

Drawn to her by joy
those progeny of hers or neighbors,
not by treats
though cookies served at each day's visits
nothing special,
just the party they deserve for being there,
and served on flowered plates with Koolaid drinks
the colors of the giant crayon box,
all sweet as the delight she showers on them
for their simply being.
Yet which boomerangs to balance off
her years of loneliness and loss.

Dichotomy

for ma soeur

She dressed fair me in softest blue; you, true brunette in red
although in manners and in learning set us on the selfsame track.
She prided having taught her genius girls to read so early
but I picture moments of her tending lovingly our dad
as you spelled out the words for me, and so I learned.

Yes, surely it was she who took us, far too small
to see over the counter at the stern librarian
disdainful of our mother's so misguided vanity
until we read for her and qualified and waved our shiny cards,
leaving the sentinel of bookshelves there to ponder
if we'd somehow cheated on her reading test.

Yet it is you I see so clear in memory, not mother,
up the stairs and steering, leading dawdler me
to fairy tales there, revelations, magic far beyond
our Bobbsey Twins at home and their puerile exploits.
So having read them all yourself at five, of course,
you left me as Snow White to floor-sit bears and princes,
Rose Red, you strode off to Scarlet Pimpernels and Gunga Dins,
sure next day to impress our somewhat less-read teaching nuns.

But later that superiority, so bright, so sure of being right,
would come to bite you, for when you spoke up, correcting them,
they charged you with, not just assurance, but with arrogance,
and with their God-dubbed righteous jealousy
denied you recognition, and the prizes you had earned.

Whatever closed you off, if it was that injustice
or the space our father left when fate betrayed us,
even as your heart fled, seeking hibernation,
still the eager, urgent mind issued demands.
You mastered spit-spot parenthood, obsessing over
mastery of crochet, crosswords, cutthroat card-play,
then resurfaced as the guru to more fractured friends. Yes, Della.
For despite your wisdom, she imploded still and left you stunned.

You remained, mind-clutched, but with your heart in full retreat.
To feel, yet blot out that reality, you sat--
Oh, more than once I see you there,
your daughters, one, two, three, four,
chairs set up as semi-circled audience to view,
not movie magic "Carousel" rerun on Channel nine, but you.
Enthralled and reassured, to see that rarity--their mother cry.

When mate abandonment almost induced despair
you new escaped to mind redeeming scholarship,
though then at last to blessed love. A mate almost your match
at least in brilliance and assurance, here an anchor more secure
and with a matching penchant for martini easing respite,
yet for you, a path to fierce agoraphobic jeopardy.

For truth will out, and when we are not wary, sister mine,
these steel-trap minds can snap shut on us, inescapable,
and keep us hostage, hearts held tight in total bondage.

Fate, though, owes some small amends to us:
The hearts our children and their children bring can peek in,
find what's hidden there, peer through the bars
and recognize our longing, reverence what we've kept
long buried. Then their love in turn can break tenfold the hold
Of mind-blind steel to reawaken in us all our heartheld tenderness.

OF PROGENY

Bond

Perhaps there is a farther sky
though I am fond of this one,

Farther gods
though I am bound to those I've known
Or possibly a nether world
As grand as this I love,

Yet never in the furthest reaches of my thought
can I conceive a wonder of more worth
than that borne of this world,
this earth, this womb.

Apologia II

Could I but trace my mind through all its mazes
could I but grace the world with gentler face
I might not need this subtle rationale
the conscience compensation of a plea.

But having never quite gone past the preaching
of the saint I should have wished myself to be
nor even the antithesis, of bluntness,
grand Mephistophelian honesty,

No--- having snubbed these opportunities
I settle for one small redeeming gift:
Self--- I know I do not treat you well
I know that
Friends--- I know I do not give enough
I know
Child--- I never mean you harm
but my goodwill is often spare
I know.

Yet each of you, believe me please.
Old sleepy secret self,
resilient soothing friends,
wild boundless loving child,
(The sequence is chronology, not preference)
believe I love you,
and perhaps that all that I can offer
is to let you love me as you choose.

Though even that assessment's self-aggrandizement
I must admit--- not even that---
successfully.

Testament

On his coming of age

I know no more of where you go
than whence you came.

I only know the honor that I feel today
at having been the bough that held you briefly
 in the moments just before you set your course
and flew.

Exchange

John Ciardi said 'I am well-traded'
in his poem I found
when you were in my womb.
Somehow I knew that boded well.

And it has proven true
in partnering, in parenting,
in loving friends whose testament confirms,
and so in me, the growth that had to be,
all led by light you held.

That splendid you,
who will not simply fill but still illuminate
the space my spirit leaves behind.

Algorithm

The poem I wrote my son at 21
was "On His Coming of Age."
Of course.
 So logical.

But he's turned 63 today.
Life cycles are absurd.
My own old age makes perfect sense.

But his?
For him, the verb 'to age'
does not compute.

5th Command

The father, briefly daddy
never really dad
tapped in from time to time
with alternate indulgence and contempt.

Once grown, you'd try
from time to time to reach
but finally cut free.

Five decades hence,
you changed his bed for him,
turned the once giant-looming body,
turned from the brilliant now diminished mind
gone so awry and let the blistering insults fall away,
returned a jibe from time to time, or laughed.

Six thousand miles from family you had built,
you simply--not so simply--served the undeserving.
But from whom in darkest night,
for just a moment full aware of unearned grace,
the voice would whisper *I do love you, son.*

Helpmate

for Aleksandra

I never knew just what that term meant--
seemed demeaning, like a housemaid, or a crutch,
accoutrement to some upstanding man.

Then when she swept into our lives,
a beauty far too fine for ordinary wear,
her bright new oh, so dazzling light
outshone each gift we tendered,
even the white roses sent to welcome her.

Still, as the years progressed,
although the beauty never faded
she would wear the habit of the harried mom,
the housemaid even, and each day
the shoulder where her weary mate might rest.

It took the night she chose to sleep, unbidden,
on the ground beside him in the park
to guard his project there
that I saw beauty clearly and could understand
what helpmate truly means.

Today a haku lei surrounds her face,
pink rosed among plumeria,
but in my mind, white roses
will forevermore adorn her crown.

Artemis of the Playground

for Jessica

Four thousand years ago, for killing of one deer,
ten thousand men were kept for years
from seizing Troy, from human killing fields.

how this one goddess,
heartsick when her creatures
were attacked, withstood the will
of Agamemnon, of Achilles,
all the might of Greece,
how she could hold Aeolus back—
no wind, no war, without amends.
Her adamance remains a wonder.

Just so, this young girl feels the pain
of frailer friends or foes
from arrowed words,
and with the gentlest of rebukes,
becalms these childhood gusts
that seed the winds of war.

Commencement

Without immunity,
armed only with our love and honor,
she who wept heartbroken once at frowns
steps now into the sweet toxicity of independence,
marshalling her white soul-cells, a ready antidote
to any venom masquerading as a path to paradise.

Prospecting

    for A.J.

Through his hands they flow,
stones, mud and sand,
churned by the force
of streams sent scurrying
by snows on melting snows
to reach the distant sea,
and be renewed.

So punishing his hands, the stream,
the cold shout:
"Move. Out of my way! Can't stop
my destiny!"
Still, sort he will,
and question every grain that passes
through his sieve: "Are you? Is this
the glitter, or the gold? The keeper?"

Hour by hour he bends to scrutinize,
his back a half-forgotten ache.
So young, this prospector,
already seeking nuggets, panning
for the brightest truth.

Legacy

I thought the only grandson ought to visit, view the brain of his
 great-granddad.
Otherwise why had he landed at that very university the selfsame
 month
as the collection, the bequest of the famed surgeon?

How much better off the boy would be, though, could he contemplate
the mind, the soul, or just the bounteous heart of this forebear.
But those went with him, for my mother would not yield a single
 gram more
of that body---of that man---she had so loved.

The Smoothers

Our grandmothers at tables
oceans distant from each other
stroked the edges of the tablecloth
the self same gesture slow repeated.

Widows years from childbearing
all unaware that still their fingers sought
to soothe the father's anger, tribulations,
colicked souls of sons, of daughters
lost to restless alien worlds.

Smoothing, smoothing, knuckles
now too gnarled to sew, crochet,
to purl the pain away with mittens,
buntings, afghans, comforters,
to pet the baby's fevered face,
undo the snarls around our secret fears.

Smooth strokes to keep our world
from crumbling,
so protect us that one day
we might come home to sit at table
with them, sip some tea and rock
and stroke the tablecloth.

Loves

Cocktail Party

I cross the room
avoid the lecherous eyes
find one or two who talk
with minds not mouths--
sometimes of you--
and I long to leave.

There is no one here
to be precious to.

White Elephants

From house to house we went prop-gathering
bits and pieces of faded lives.
A great backyard green overgrowth
untended by the lady but god-fed,
his fatted calf whose last meal she would be.
The crazy antique shop the NY tough had taken on
stuck off all country-hilled
no longer nagged by time cards, subway trains
his own boss, mauling porcelain and glass.
A maze of house sprawled out hodge podge
by generations all of whom it seemed by count
must still be there, and fields that billowed
so you felt you'd bounce if you should run.

From house to house to all these characters
each one as much like bric-a-brac to me
as any scavenged love seat,
my man related all his life, his fears and dreams
spewed out his soul while I sat agonized.
I watched these strangers melt into his friends
as silently I sipped my lemonades
and scorned and envied every one
but most the warmth and openness
of this, a man I loved,
for seeing them meet eyes and lives,
I knew I was the only oddity.

Trip

In view of the fact that so few of my facets
have ever excited the slightest man's prayer
I think it appalling though ego enthralling
to find myself suddenly where,
though an instant before I am caught in the throes
of a thoroughly, horribly anguished ennui,
I am suddenly stopped by a moment's digression
to find your eyes worshiping me.

Green Lilacs

I saw our love at first
as one takes sudden notice of green lilacs.

Now, though the fullness of the blossoms
with their glory of new whiteness
and its heady breath of spring
have come, do come at intervals,
yet always somewhere in my soul
I'll see you new.

You will forever be for me
that first fresh moment of surprise
discovering green lilacs.

Spring

Yesterday when I was born and saw
the first last face I ever hope to see
such laughter caught and shook me
that it burst the last of my cocoon.

I took great breaths
and giddy on the rarer air
walked earth with you
as though it were a trampoline,
flew flower to flower with you
as if we'd never need to rest.

Yet is it any wonder that today I shiver
with the chill of knowing
I shall nevermore be chrysalis.

Parallel Lines

Your lashes brush my skin from distances
and leave it burned
as though you'd scraped your beard
along my cheek.

Caress me with your eyes again.
These flames may teach me yet
to speak in human tongues.

Mind's Eyes

I have stopped, almost, regretting what we won't,
all the have nots to waste or the haves to want not.
Besides, I know them.
I do.

If I think of you very hard, for instance, very hard
I can crinkle your hair with the corners of my eyes
and set it down with your head in it
find your eyes and catch you smiling at me
across my pillow.
True.

Or when the light is right too early in the morning
I can bathe in you, but only if I'm nude.
I mean suns, if mind's eyes are at all good,
must be undressed for, no? Not on the highway though.
Policemen never understand.
I do.

And some very dark nights, long of winter ones
you make them endless Zeus-nights,
masquerade as Bacchus, all barefooted and goat-footed
being all you want and I of woman.
And I never turn into a swan.
Never.

But best, whenever I look closely, as more and more
I do, at children, yours and mine but even others',
I can close my eyes and find our children.
Found, they are.
True.

Which is the reason why I've stopped, almost, regretting.

In Concert

You are not here.
She is, I am.
I listen,
watching her perform
in costume almost me,
Antigone,
and wonder could it be
subconsciously selected.

I hear you in a tone she plays.
She floats you to me
on a chord of strings,
 the bond now tenuous,
now tensile.
And it chills me
that we three should be united so
in concert.

Breakfast

Their eyes accept me,
just as much a fixture
as the poaching egg.

Perhaps I too am poaching.
But why should it matter?
Just a little salt
and we are palatable.

Papa seasons well.

Communication

There is some power of proximity
essential or coincidental,
which one is hard tell,
to talking, really talking to you.

And this sunder thing
that happens that I hate,
although at times it may be separation
distances in scores of miles,
still other times it seems like
just the absence of a table
or the angle that our shoulders form.
A few degrees too little or too much
resets the note.

Yet see the pattern
stubbornly refusing to be set.
I've spoken at your feet or at your side.
The table may be merely accident.

But as I ponder it I wonder,
if I placed our chairs just so,
perhaps we'd talk forever.

Red Stamps

You ration out your love
and yet I buy,
deluded
that the whole economy
is on a wartime scale.

For Such a Man

In you I sought unceasingly
to find a man for every season.
You declined to be.

And still I hesitate to seek
a man somewhere for spring
and one for fall
one man for winter
one for summer,
men for each and every season,
when in truth they may be
only you by fourths.

2000 Days

The night that we first came together
as the skeptic in me speculated on our going on
you kissed my wrist, assured me,
Girl, tomorrow is another day.

And so it was.
The sun and moonlight followed us
four hundred days of wine and adulation
lavished on each other.

Then all too soon the storm and gloom of nights
of midnight calls, of doubting you as you would go
to drag her back from threats of suicide, manipulation.
I would cling and you would stroke my hair
and reassure me with, remember now,
Tomorrow is another day.

And so it was.
As back you came
all puppy-penitent and eager, passionate
and I'd succumb to one more day
that turned to fifteen hundred more.

And when our fifth year ended with her gone,
you found her surrogate to slake your need
to feed my jealousy, that drunk, despairing,
I would call and wake you, weep
and you would yawn and say, you know
about tomorrow. It's another day.

And so I did.
And so it was, for in he came,
the red beard of my poet dream,
who'd shared my dreams
some twenty years before, before the beard.

So when you phoned
that same 2000th day,
I told you I would go with him.
And you were stunned, bereft, and I could say,
Tomorrow is another life.

My Maine

Be with me, love, for you have summer fields of beard
and johnny-jump-up cornflower eyes
such hands as tempt the sprout
or heal the hearts of chilly chickadees
or set deep fence posts for us
firm as sentinels against all aliens.

The wonder of your wit can play the jester
just to tickle all my snarls away.

Because your mind holds lakes and seas
and lets your eyes reflect them
and because my coastal rocks are lodged
full measure in your loyalty,
for all of these this year of limbo is not lost.

You are my Maine, my seasons,
I am home.

Options

What can you do in six short days:

You can erode a rock
or polish it a bit,
indent a sand dune
or engrave it, slightly too,
puncture a wall
or even a trust, a tiny hole.

So small a hole,
surely it can be patched.
That is, if you can find
and put your finger on it.

The Book insists you can create a world:
I wonder rather
 if you can destroy one.

Friday Lost

A bleary eye alone marks off the moment
sequence lost of youdid Idid youdidnot
or I was not.

You go to bed for respite.
 I remain
to listen to the nothing
of the youdid Idid nothing
to the something that we somehow
doing nothing killed.

Pan, Unmasked

Red beard lover of life
a friend of beasties, women, men,
sea greeter spirit welcomer,
soother of pain, server of needs.
All these.

And still,
the secret keeper of the need
to selfishly be soothed and served
and full adored,
lest he regress and bare
his cloven heart.

The Rock

Our phallic bird has gone to ply the deeper water,
gulls who envied us our mouths upon each other pass aloof,
and only terns fly by to mock my solitude with cries.

Here comes the little man; he wonders where you are
but does not ask. He saw how wholly one we were
the day he spoke . He calls
Hello, you like the sun, eh?
I reply and he abandons me.

It seems that we were never here at lowest tide.
The crevice where you set your feet is dry
and like the shells it holds
I feel so terribly exposed.

The cradle of the risen water and our unity
now having gone,
I am unsheltered on this rock
that I had thought our fortress.

Light

The sun is more intense today
the water glitters brighter by the hour
at night the bathroom bulb
the candles in the living room
the stars the fire all glow
as clearly as on Thursday last.

You see, since you have gone
only my inner light has dimmed a bit.

Mediation: Heron

Between the dark and light lies truth,
so even as I listen to the massive falsehood
wonder at the callousness beneath,
I must remember that you tendered me
the other great blues too.

Settled In

As I look up and up the pillar, neck extended so,
I laugh and realize in moving I felt settled
only with that presence at my back.
It's so the way I choose to sit with men I need,
to lean on masculinity.

Four pillars front me now,
I've shifted as the sun has.
They elongate their shadows but I am not taken in,
I know the pillar at my back suffices.
Shadows do not comfort or support.

I should remember that,
not try to lean on those
who turn out to be shadows.

Seedbed

Weep and reap what's sown
lie easy or uneasy
unmade beds give no reproach
and fallow fields chide seldom.

But when all is done
admit you'd rather know
you've made a furrow
than remained aloof
unmussed, unfertilized.

Worlds

Hometown

Kenya

Maine

Here

HOMETOWN

Irish Ides

Our caravan keeps movin'
getaway, no way
no floats in this parade
except for Johnny's soul.
His Irish eyes ain't smilin' now
as flat as jade they're starin' at the desert sun,
no wearin' of the green fatigues
just tan to blend with sand
except that rusty hole in him.
The truck speeds up
and bloody drops of Johnny fly off,
ploppin' in the sand behind
each raisin' puffs of dust
like little celebrations
promises, rememberin's--

Acchh, how he couldn't wait,
this Johnny that I hardly knew,
to get there, couldn't wait then to get home
to be here for The Day—on 43rd Street--
Green beer pitchers, all the vets
old chins a-quiver, quaverin' voices
callin' up the emerald isle
Ol' Donegal and Galway Bay.
Forgottin' for that day
the long months, years
at the Ardennes, Khe Sanh,
at Seoul, the endless days
of rottin' teeth and rotten feet--

Ah, no, he couldn't wait, just to get home
and see that crew, his boys
aah, not his kids, his station mates
to tell our tales,
them dusty promises.

And up now from our guts
come all the bile,
green poison fed us
that we swallowed--
All their Toora Looras
Toora Loora, Toora Loora Lies
on lies on lies.

October Nightmare

My home was not assailed, but too adjacent,
yet I find no comfort in the rifles aimed
so diligently by my doors.

My stained glass windows never offered threats;
the water lilies, amaryllis, set no false alarms.
But I am fringed by hate on hate,
this nest of peace surrounded,
my survival resting anxiously on how much
who hates whom tonight and where.

So I check in
past boys in uniforms they've donned too hastily
to wear with ease,
and having soothed the siren-stricken dog,
check out, to seek more peaceful homes than mine.

Although they have no water lilies,
neither have they rifles,
so will offer greater rest to me
this night of hate I cannot measure.

Requiescat

Sleep peacefully, dear neighbors,
sleep.
The radio assures us that the hate
is all contained within a four block area.

It pleases you I know
that you can rest in peace,
but just before you close your eyes,
consider
how much rage there is tonight.

How often have you taken
the cube root of rage
contained in four times four blocks?

Have you seen the face of one child
one frame three times one
absorbing rage,
or ever truly measured
rage within a father six foot two
cut off and not allowed to pass,
whose children lie within that rage?

Have you determined yet,
you almost shuttered lids,
precisely who and how you smother
as you lie encompassed by
twelve inches wide, three inches deep
of pillow-smug contentment?

KENYA

*Kwa Heri**

Old man
why do you stay?
The Kenya you loved
if ever you loved
is gone
like your wife
with the era
of blackwater fever.

*goodbye

Hygiene

And bottled water with your scotch?
My dear, you're fifty years too late.

I do regret informing you,
I know you're never out of date,
But facts are facts and water here
(Lean in – I'll whisper in your ear)
is chlorinated through and through.

Dragonflies

They come with the rains
their brittle bodies shedding
silkscreen wings,
mass upon mass
of tensile gossamer.

Maddening creatures
too gentle to kill
too stubborn to free
too corrupt to keep,
condemned
like the girls who swarm the city
to lives as bittersweet plague.

They

Who need
no more a sculptured
landscape hop the
rail and hit
the coast to ride
the sprouts that
splay the then line wheeling
over seahorse heads
ducked under
sand invasion
Splat.
They reap
an eager mouthful of
the salt stiff
generation come to terms
with sodden sea slugs
seek a mother
find a father
under coral claws,
amazed
to see the world and
be the world
in soft companioned
solitude
Beyond the reef.

Town Boys, Uganda

Great knowing eyes
return my gaze
no friendliness within
nor even curiosity
but only challenges
from these young wise.

They are the tough ones
all survivors
and I cheer them
who will never scrape
nor cower.

I cheer and wave
but they
do not wave back
and I am glad.

Verse and Response

Return my man, you long-haired white-faced whore
The voice comes down the hall
The footsteps slapping stone
You husband thief, you listen to my words
The knuckles beat a pattern on the door
(Confiteor, Confiteor)

You will not stay here now, no more
Not alive in Kenya
Not my home
You'll die or I will first, I swear to you
The rhythm of the pounding as before
(Confiteor, Confiteor)

You do not know the suffering we went through
I worked for him
I sent him to your land
What, can't you find a man as white as you
The knocking, pounding, hammering anew
(mea culpa, mea culpa)

My children cry to know where he has been—
You listen to them
Where's your soul
How dare you call yourself a Christian then
Black hands reach up to beat the door again
(mea culpa, mea culpa)

Until you leave my man or land I vow—
You won't be safe
They'll cut your head off, girl
I have my people looking for you now
The final knock, the heel clicks fading off
(mea culpa, mea maxima culpa)

The Norfolk

Grey clouds, a dusky day
a Bergman film and beer
small tables topped with copper,
Clapboard-roofed.

Content.

With all the foreign flavored savored sweet
this land has brought to me,
it's comfortable inanities like these
I may remember best.

MAINE

Inhabitants

Peaceful they are, these towns.
You can't quite place the source of such
exquisite silence till you've counted
toothless mouths and graying hairs.
They're tough, the towns, the rocks,
the people.
Talk to them.

They say the grandson stays the summer.
Well, the son-in-law he found some work
in Massachusetts.
They come up, the daughter and the kids a week
or two each year,
and then the other daughter she went off to college,
nothing for her here.
The educated can't find work,
not even many tradesmen here.
Had to go to Waterville to find a man
to put the bathroom in.
No shops to hire sales help neither
not to speak of,
just for summer none year round.
The daughter's kids—it's fine to have them visit
but they get to drive you crazy after couple weeks,
sure is peaceful when they're gone.

Well, say it's nice to talk but better get along,
got traps to check today or maybe Wednesday
if it rains this afternoon – no rush--
might fix that gutter later on.
Hope you'll like it here,
It's quiet anyhow.

Watch them give a nod and off to putter
or collect the check that slippery Roosevelt
ought never to have started
or at least that's what they voted
back when they were young and made their bargain:
Doggedly to reap the harvest of the sea
and find they'd given their posterity in trade—
but after all it may be just as well.
It's quieter that way.

The Auction

I have here a William and Mary highboy
of the period—of the period
Now this one's maple—most of the ones you'll see
that's of the period are all mahogany with all those insets fallin' apart.
Now there's a bit of a debate that
that there top is married to that bottom
that they were from two different pieces—but I ask you—
who could argue with a happy marriage?

Who'll start it at nine hundred
do I hear nine hundred
nine hundred or I'll put it by--
You're missin' the boat on this,
five thousand if it wasn't for that top and that there bottom--
Do I hear nine hundred--
Put it by.

A cherry lowboy here—American.
Mr. Bacon came into Maine last summer
and paid three thousand for a country one
that wasn't any better than this one.

I'm gonna start it at a hundred
a hundred dollars at a hundred
make it a hundred twenty five--
You biddin' there, miss? She's wavin' at everybody--
At a hundred twenty five now
a hundred twenty five call it a hundred fifty
at a hundred fifty—a hundred fifty dollars

call it a hundred seventy five
a hundred fifty call it a hundred seventy five
--I'm gonna sell it—
Last call—
Number.

There's a signed Norton pottery vase
wonderful for large bouquets and flowers
wonderful for this—wonderful for that.
It can go right in your summer house, or right in your winter house.

I'll start at fifty
fifty dollars at fifty make it sixty
at fifty dollars now call it sixty
at sixty dollars call it seventy
at seventy dollars call it eighty
eighty- ninety
at ninety dollars call it a hundred--
If you want it, bid
don't be shy there,
at ninety dollars at ninety dollars
call it a hundred
--Fair warning—
Number.

Here's a ship's clock--
There's a little wheel missin' on the striker,
it'll strike one for two bells--
It's nice—you don't have to go on watch.

Who'll start it at two hundred
I've got two hundred
two hundred now
two hundred dollars make it two hundred twenty five

two hundred twenty five call it two hundred fifty
two hundred fifty call it two seventy five
two seventy five call it three hundred dollars
three hundred dollars call it three twenty five
--Fair warning—
Three hundred dollars over there call it three
twenty five—
Number.

Now who requested this here chamber pot?
Hope ya don't need it just this minute.
They don't use these old things the same way now--
Y'know I have some friends from Texas
and they drink punch from these without the cover--

Who wants to start this off at twenty dollars
I've got twenty dollars at twenty dollars call it thirty
at twenty dollars now thirty dollars
thirty dollars call it forty
forty dollars call it fifty
fifty dollars now call it sixty
fifty dollars now make it sixty
Lotta Texas punch drinkers here
fifty dollars in the front now call it sixty--
Last call—Number.

Now here's an illustrated Bible
date on it is seventeen hundred,
lady wants to get a price on these so
I won't let it go for less than a hundred fifty.
I'm a little impressed with these nude ladies
Walkin' through the garden with the lions--
How lucky can a lion get?

Start it at a hundred fifty
I've got a hundred fifty make it a hundred seventy five
a hundred seventy five call it two hundred
two hundred dollars now call it two twenty five
two hundred while you're gossipin' makin' up your minds
two hundred make it two twenty five
No?
Fair warning—
Number.

This next there is a pair of signed pewter
miniature whale oil lamps signed Putnam American pewter.
If we can't start at three hundred dollars
I'll put 'em by--
Gentleman says they're not a matched pair
that's true they never were--people in those days were not matched either
One here has a ring around and the other doesn't
one was probably his and one was hers.

I'm gonna start 'em at three hundred
do I have three hundred
I've got three hundred call it three hundred fifty
three hundred fifty call it four
four hundred make it four hundred fifty
four fifty make it five hundred
five hundred dollars call it five hundred fifty
five hundred twenty five he makes it
five hundred twenty five call it five hundred
five hundred twenty five make it five hundred fifty
--I'm gonna sell it—
Last call—Number.

That's enough—I'm tired—Bob, take over.

Pine Groves

Beyond, there is the forest where the tune is heavier.
I never leave a pine grove with the feeling
I bring into it. It's disillusioning.
Out in the meadow insects serenade, but inside
secret bogs below the needles harbor gnats, mosquitoes,
all too interested in me. And being less a masochist
than I'm inclined to think I am, I skitter out
with little more than one perfunctory breath.
Expecting chapel coolness is the major error.
Pine groves sometimes disappoint you.

I longed for years to own a pine grove,
made love once in one. We'd driven out
oh, earlier than this but end of summer,
still it felt the same as this day's sun
or this day's air, or maybe only of the absence coming.
At any rate I'd opened up my shirt to feel the wind,
though really that was consequence, not purpose,
so we drove the narrow road until the pine grove showed
around the bend and hardly thinking of it knew it was for us.
We didn't for a moment touch except our hands
and then got rid of other interferences.
When we had loved the heat was heavy; bites already tingled
under sweat, and we were happier back on the road
with breeze and movement.
Pine groves, as I say, can disappoint you.

Round Pond

When he was seven we first found the village.
Lobstering and sea fog, rocks and oddities
none finer than the old man who still walked
miles of the road each day and raised a hand
to greet the cars of his familiars.

So that summer and some seven following
we were admitted to the ranks of greeted.
Every summer driving in we'd see him wave
and know we had arrived.

Some twenty years had passed
before our separate journeys brought us back.
and driving in we thought of the old walker,
As we turned the corner, shocked to see ahead
a frail bent body coming. Could it be—
No—he'd be near a hundred now.

It was, and coming near we waved
just wild like children out both windows,
waved and yelled "Hi, oh, hello!" Elated.
But he never raised his head or eyes,
kept both tuned to the ground as we passed by.

And driving on, it was as if some breath
Had left the car. Then in the rear view mirror
saw receding, like the past itself, his figure
and the old hand slowly rise up, filling
both our eyes, my grown up boy's and mine.

HERE

The Aina

Reply to Robert Frost

We were the land's before the land was ours
when centuries and continents ago
we curled in misery
to sleep, to see such visions.

Placid waters roiled to rapids robbing shores
and awesome reaches that evoked in us such power
that though no gods, so set our minds
to feeling worthy of the land that we refused
to recognize that we were merely tenants.

Owned ourselves, no owners, we'd deny the truth:
The glory always was and is the land's;
the dream we dreamed alone belongs to us.

Faith

I went out yesterday
to watch a whale or two,
but there were none.

I still believe in whales.

I question only
whether they believe in me.

Sideswiped

I grew up today
saw bright new metal crumple
stopped and thought me,
Save your griefs
you'll need them, every one.

Not one regret.
A thing
not dog, not home
not husband, mother, child
but just a pretty thing
as easy come as easy gone,
not worth the vial to waste
an honest tear upon.

Orchestration

I hate to ride the bus,
leery of bunched up people
but today I must.

I breathe the standees sweat
am thrust between a bleating teen
her pink phone grasped:
"You din't…I seen you wit' her!
Yeah, you did. You suck!"

And to my right a blue ear-budded
bloated wanna be
barks out his faux prestige:
"Well, fuck'em! If they can't deliver,
Fire their asses. Yeah, I said so!"

All my glowers, sighs, stink eyes
have no impact.
(And if they did, might he—or she—attack me?)

Never mind.
Instead, I tuck my head
and read my book.
Aloud.
Composed,
in perfect dissonance.

Reflections

Warmups

Portraits

Ponderings

WARMUPS

Transformation

> What one has ever loud proclaimed
> that being chrysalis was comfortable?

True Love

> What cricket ere complained
> of mate who talked too much?

Coast Town

> He has two teeth to her none.
> Yet how he reveres her.

Beachgoers

> Let's all go 'round looking dotty,
> shall we not'y?

Quelle?

> Ah, phone, why must you keep on ringy-dingling
> when I'm on the potty tinkling?

Teen Spring

> Sprouts of orange in brunette tresses,
> shorter'n shorter'n shorter dresses.

PORTRAITS

First Day

They mean so well
with all their foolish grumblings.
Despite the slanted shoulder of defense
they mean today so well, so much to be their best.

Their will may falter, shred tomorrow
but I wonder only this--
From whom they learned to mean so well,
so very well, today.

Life Study: Sam

The chair becomes a pedestal
where framed but never molded,
angles in black wire,
he sits like some conceived
but soon abandoned sculpture.

Shoulder blades poke brittle
through the shirt that covers not enough
those stunted fragile arms he hides
beneath the desk.

But as I pass
his eyes belie unfinished limbs
and will me to believe him whole.

Resilience

for Lynne

The curve of silver waves around her face,
a lightest lilt of voice,
the modest deprecation of her artist's gift,
and the agape love she wears as her loose garment--
  Whispers, all these, somehow of fragility.

Yet, as true silk once woven
masks its tensile strength,
so she prevails--
A testament to gossamer.

Grace

Good habits foster grace:
Her birthday book, kept faithfully,
engendered greetings, fine handwritten
like the thank you notes she wrote, on time.

Whenever we'd come by, the lights came on,
especially in her eyes.
We'd smile, she'd cook
and serve us waffles with more wit than syrup.

And if later of those Sunday afternoons, she tippled
as she worked the double crossword
and forgot and scorched the green beans,
spilled her drink perhaps, or then herself,
well, who could fault so dear a soul?

Except perhaps her consort spouse
who had, she'd whispered,
put the bottle down for good, for her,
those many years before,
lest when their child was born, she'd toss him out.

Who'd smile and take her hand and help her up,
Yet in whose eyes her light would dim
with each succeeding week, each year,
Sunday by Sunday.

Pre- Post Prandials

She pours the gin to melt her icy crust
so she can say she loves me
and she does once more
and then again, and once again
till I demur, and pour my own.

A little bubbly, and a little more
perhaps some more still
after all it's really celebration
life that is and us both here,
a paradise to keep the world all sparkling
keep the beastly blemishes,
especially ours, at bay.

Swimmer

Later than autumn he dreams of youth
his muscles now more taut in August's sea
than mountain streams could ever make them
when his veins held spring.

To an Analyst

I knew a poet once
who could not look another person in the eye
whose gaze would wince and wander
founder like a sailboat with its ballast lost.

I wondered then why should a man
who could expose his soul to readers' eyes
still fear to meet the gaze of anyone.

So much I wondered that at last I realized
I too averted eyes, and I suspect
that was, as much as phobias of empty house,
what drew me lumbering to you.

Only to find, as fears of darkness
week by week are driven to your wall,
so often are my eyes.

Emperorang

Those graspy little paws pose far less threat
than do your imprimatur dictum-decrees
on not only economics and diplomacy
but faith and [sic] morality

As if your little hour to strut and fret
upon our stage with tarnished crown
bestows infallibility in these
and all the matters that may bind us
till the longed for blessed moment
that your tired tweets are heard no more.

Imported Beauty's Vow

For such a name, I'll leave my family
and take your multi-mothered ones as mine,
abandon girlhood dreams of my own worth
to gather yours around me like a cloak.
For such a name, I'll kill the longing soul
that screams inside my mind for freedom,
trust your land gives all I'll see of light
and that your wealth can fill this need in me.

Your power can afford what I must have,
no matter what they say the cost to me;
I will give all I cherish of myself
to be the woman you display—and keep.
Yet comes on now the echo, and repeats:
Be careful what you wish for, sweet.

Shoddy Product

I am reversible--
on one side, even waterproof.
But sometimes I'll forget
and try to wear my inside out
in less than clement weather.
Shameful how I shrink!

Energy Crisis

The jaw is but the hinge
upon which hinges what I speak
so should you hear my verses squeak,
pray do not be alarmed.
Dismiss it as a shortage
of some intellectual lubricant.

Waterborne

I swim.
Age twelve to thirteen, every night I swam the dream,
each night the same, the shock, the bliss, as at the door,
What! Daddy? But you are....
I thought you knew...I was off working in Alaska, Africa,
Arabia, in Timbuktu--
And oh, the celebrating then--just a mistake!
But swam awake to loss again each morning,
till the day I swam the dream no more
when in my inmost being I could say *No, no mistake.*

Then swam the other losses, loves and cherished dreams,
and even hard against the tide, the mother rip tide
when the boy said he would stay in India,
I treaded water till my deepest self accepted
Yes, and possibly for good. They can't be us,
and could exult then on the shore when he came home.

Marriage washed away to pull me under,
years submerged in drink and struggling
underneath the waves of bitterness,
to finally encounter creatures of the sea like me
but who had reached the surface,
found that they could breathe again,
and in their wake learned that my lungs could fill again.

I swim today one-lunged, but strong
from other laps, those other struggles,
lesson learned *Of course, whether I live or not,
my world will be all right.*
So, lifetimes later, backstroking, I watch the sky
and bask in beauty every day I swim.

Zara, Year One

You were a vision, clearly proved by photos, videos
though certainly too perfect to be real.

No, no we weren't deluded, our own awe confirmed
by friends who saw our plethora of posted you-views.
Cheering for your light, they felt its afterglow and clamored
for yet more, addicted like us, to your images.

When finally you came to visit our domain,
we played the fools, and uttered noises
not a single earthly creature ever made,
and waved, blew kisses, little-piggy'd
long before they'd mean a thing to you.
Then shocked we were, astounded by your brilliance
when secretly you mastered and returned
such wondrous universal human signs.

For grow you will, you do, to our delight, dismay.
Each month a gain, a loss--the former greater, true
but pain still, knowing baby moments flee
not to be seen again by us except in memory,
or the perfect picture with your paper crown askew
that says good morning and good night each day.

One truth remains, reminds us that these smiles,
your luminescent joy, are not lost to the stars
but tucked away and lodged there in your being
all the days that you may grace the world.

PONDERINGS

Reply to Bobby Burns

O wad some Power the giftie gie us
To see oursels as ithers see us!

And then the courage
time and bucks
for dermabrasion
nips and tucks!

Exposure

The finest writers show what's under
their emotional underwear.

Just doff that bra, its underwires
faux lifting up the droop of smiles
both natural and contrived,
that hide the pain of loneliness,
and too, the stuffing, pads to fill out
all the gaps of empathy.

And are those Spanx, m'dear?
Do you believe they keep the secret
of the greed and envy
 that so comfort you ?

Now strip those briefs.
as if they could conceal the fears,
the hidden guilt, the shame
you claimed to shed.

Sweet freedom beckons--
come be naked in the world,
all daring with your beauty and your flaws!

We'll wait while you undress.

Proprietary Rights

The Play Spirit that conjured macadamia nuts,
orgasms, malamutes and mangoes,
oceans, eyes and synapses--
That spirit sowed no seeds of armament,
no envy pollen, hate buds,
no greed-endings to the nerves,
much less an inbred longing for the song of war.

These weapons are our own--
invented, crafted with keen wit
and replicated by our arrogance.
Therein we hold sole patent,
fiercest guard to these,
the precious seeds of our extinction.

Exempt

Even the trees, we hear, can wince
and mourn and warn of threat.

Yet here in humankind
some suffer anhydrosis
such that seared skin, sliced flesh,
even splintered limb
may go unnoticed even as they sleep.

Others of us, more than those,
feel body pain, but are afflicted
with immunity to psychic pain.

In us, the scorching of the soul,
the shattered heart,
such mortal wounds may strike
without our recognition or response.

Oh, to be healed of each disease
that like our fellows, like the trees,
we may at least with each relentless blow of fate
experience that rich release--the howl of grief.

Universal Blessing

on Dump Road

Spirit in Us, bless the stones, rocks, trees,
the pruners and the planters, trucks and ship lanes,
litterers and littered, all those safe or threatened,
bless the taro, weeds, white ginger,
red tape, politicians, rebels, passions, joys and griefs.

All the feral pigs and cats and dogs in fierce pursuit,
their masters, caring or indifferent, bless them,
and the sinister or ambidextrous, idols, dreamers,
scholars, laggards, saints and fritterers,
the lost, deluded or despairing.

Bless the brutalized now brutal, all the lovers, haters,
baffled, full of blood lust, living and half-living,
all the dead, embrace their bodies, spirits,
and our memories of them,
each in turn, with full regard, be blessed,
lest we relinquish our humanity entirely.

Jan Shiarella McGrath | *Author*

Born Janice Champagne in upstate New York, I scrambled to keep up with my accomplished elder sister. My love of learning that resulted, especially for literature and theater, led me through SUNY Albany, Penn State U., U.C. Nairobi, and U. Maine's 3 campuses. Teaching high school and college students, aspiring adults and those imprisoned, brought greater joy in poetry, both the encouraging and writing of it. My passion for acting and play writing held most of my creative attention, which earned recognition. But so had poetry writing, and I kept returning always to its lure. That love led me now to glean this small selection from drawers full of poems, older and new. Because I trust my work is accessible to all readers, I hope the poems bring some satisfaction to you, as they have to me.

Anita Benson | *Artist & Illustrator*

My grandfather said that I was an artist when I was four years old, and I've been drawing and painting ever since. I was awarded a Master's Degree from California State College, Chico in both painting and Art History in 1980. I taught Drawing, Watercolor and Art Appreciation for almost 20 years at Monterey Peninsula College in CA, and Figure Drawing at Pacific Grove Art Center, CA. I have illustrated five children's books, and one Science Fiction graphic novel. After living in Hawaii for 16 years, I relocated to Arizona. Excited there by the new visuals which inspired my work, I am now moving to an island off Thailand. Life is an adventure we must chase.

Acknowledgments

Several of the Kenya poems appeared in the East African Publishing anthology *Faces at Crossroads*. Other poems previously published include "Apologia II," in the journal *Voices International*, and "Smoothers" in *Hawaii Pacific Review*.

Special gratitude goes to those who gave generous time and encouragement as my readers--memoir author Joan Kelleher, poet Timothy Dyke, Margaret Pearlman, and Carol Egan. Many thanks to fellow writer Carol Polcovar, at whose urging I finally took on the task of gleaning this collection, and to Anita Benson, an artist whose work awes me, for agreeing to be my illustrator. I am indebted in all my writing work to the NLAPW Pen Women of Honolulu, and to the inspiration of my spirit sisters of Na Wahine o Koolau, especially Jocelyn, Suzanne, Margaret, and Sara.

Thanks to Colin Rolfe at Epilogue/Monkfish for again guiding me through the maze of publishing. The greatest debt, of course, is to my son John Narayan, who has made me happy always to continue living and writing.

www.ingramcontent.com/pod-product-compliance
Lightning Source LLC
Chambersburg PA
CBHW021014090426
42738CB00007B/779